Beyond the Tranquil Blue

Whispers from the Depths of the Soul

Sampad Dutt

BookLeaf Publishing
India | USA | UK

Made with ❤ on the BookLeaf Publishing Platform
www.bookleafpub.in
www.bookleafpub.com

For the precious few who have been my steady ground and quiet light, through every joy and heartbreak. You have taught me to embrace life's beauty and fragility with open arms. This book is my offering of gratitude and love, an attempt to capture what words cannot express. It is dedicated to you, with all I am.

Acknowledgement

Creating this poetry collection has been a deeply personal and transformative journey, and I owe immense gratitude to those who have been part of it.

To my mother and friends: your unwavering encouragement has been my greatest strength. Your love has given me the courage to take risks and share my innermost thoughts with the world.

To my mentors and fellow writers: thank you for your invaluable feedback and guidance. Your insights helped me grow as a poet, and I am forever grateful for the wisdom and perspective you have shared.

To all the authors whose work has inspired me: your artistry has illuminated the beauty of the written word. Your work has profoundly impacted my understanding of poetry. Thank you for showing me what is possible within its form.

And finally, to you, the reader: thank you for engaging with this collection. I hope these poems resonate with your own experiences and emotions, creating a connection that bridges our worlds.

With deepest appreciation,
Sampad

Preface

In the pages that follow, you will find a collection of poems reflecting my journey through love, loss, and the kaleidoscope of emotions that color our existence. Each piece is a fragment of my heart, a moment suspended in time, capturing the beauty and pain of life's unpredictable path.

Love, grief, and healing are universal forces that shape us in profound ways, often beyond the reach of words. In the heart of human experience, these forces carve circles within us, tracing stories of passion, pain, and perseverance. This anthology seeks to explore these stories through the lens of the seven stages—each a testament to the emotional landscapes we navigate in our most vulnerable and transformative moments.

Our journey begins with love. It leads us from the spark of attraction to a deeper unity, as we surrender to forces beyond our control.

The stages of love—each more intense and consuming than the last—mirror the phases of a flame, kindling and blossoming, until it envelopes the spirit.

What follows us is grief, a shadow cast in the absence of love, and sets a pall of gloom over our lives. The stages of grief are pathways carved by loss, yet through them, we learn the language of resilience. Each stage becomes a chapter in learning to coexist with ache, honoring what we've lost while cherishing what remains.

Finally, we arrive at the journey of rediscovery and redemption. Through these stages, the heart seeks not only reunion but a renewal of purpose and meaning. It is a return, not to what was, but to a place of acceptance and clarity, where love is redefined in its purest essence.

Each poem in this collection invites you to immerse yourself in three intertwining journeys. These verses are an open invitation for you to explore the connections we share, to recognize echoes of your own experiences within my words. Poetry possesses a unique power to bridge the gaps between souls, reminding us that our struggles and joys are universal.

As you read, I hope you uncover fragments of yourself within these lines—moments that resonate with your own path. May these poems offer solace, ignite inspiration, and cultivate a sense of belonging. Thank you for joining me on this adventure, where language and emotion weave together, and mirth and merriment marries the crests and troughs of life.

Yours truly,
Sampad

Enchantment

She is a fragment of dawn, a splinter of
stardust,
A silhouette upon the shadowed tapestry of
evening.
Her presence is a quiet implosion,
A radiance folded into mystery,
And I am caught, suspended in the orbit of
her gaze.
Her eyes—dark wells rimmed with
moonlight,
Force me to delve deep into them, as
explorers often do, amidst the boundless seas,

Holding the uncharted depths of unseen worlds,
And her lips, a whisper of ancient verses,
Etched upon my senses, delicate as morning dew.
To look upon her is to savour the birth
Of something vast, unnamed, infinite—
A flame at the edge of knowing,
Soft yet insistent, drawing me closer, closer as ever.
She is neither dream nor flesh alone;
She is a constellation veiled in silk and shadow.
A stranger, yet the compass of my desires,
A vision that lingers, like a sacred secret.
Her beauty speaks in the stillness,
And I am silenced, entranced,
As though the heavens themselves
Had whispered her into being,
And she, simply, let me gaze at her.

Embrace

She dwells now within me, her spirit threaded
Through every fold of thought, every pulse of
breath.
I trace the lines of her in daybreak,
In the still hours when dawn meets quiet
earth,
And I am seized by an exquisite yearning,
Sweet and unyielding as the pull of the sea.
Her laughter is the song of rivers unseen,
Her voice a gentle murmur in the quiet heart
of night.
She moves as water graced by moonlight,
Each step a tender revelation, each glance a
poem.
Her skin is woven from twilight and embers,

A softness the stars might envy, aglow from within.
I am drawn to her, a man undone, enthralled,
Captured by the intangible, lost in her shadow.
The scent of her lingers, haunting and divine,
And I hold it like a relic, precious, fleeting.
For she has entered my soul like a fevered prayer,
And I am cast adrift, a willing wanderer.
I know her name as intimately as the ache in my bones,
And to love her feels like surrender—
An endless fall into the boundless beauty that is her.

Longing

I love her, and this love is a tempest,
A sacred fury bending all reason to its will.
She is fierce beauty, she is wild grace,
A tempest carved from the fire of creation itself.
Her eyes are obsidian mirrors, ancient and boundless,
Where the mysteries of the night are born and kept.
She is the fire and the sea, the very breath of earth,
Her laughter, a song lifted on the wings of fate.

To be near her is to stand at the edge of infinity,
to feel both the solace and terror of all things vast.
Her hands are rivers where I willingly drown,
Her skin, an expanse of silken twilight.
In her presence, I am stripped bare,
A man surrendered, consumed by a force beyond flesh.
She does not merely live;
She inhabits every fragment of my being,
An unyielding pulse, an ever-beating heart.
And I, a pilgrim to her uncharted lands,
Am humbled beneath the weight of her gaze.
This love is no longer mine; it is hers,
A gift given freely, completely, without end.
For she is my compass, my burning star,
And to love her is to finally know the beauty of my own ruin.

Divinity

In her I find a sanctuary carved from quiet strength,
A fortress where shadows dare not linger.
She is both earth and sky, boundless yet grounded,
Her beauty shaped by the unyielding stones of resolve.
Her eyes are the color of rivers at dusk,
Deep and unwavering, holding the truth of things.
To stand beside her is to know the grace of mountains,
Silent, enduring, ancient in their vigil.
I rest my soul upon the contours of her kindness,

Knowing she cradles my fears as gently as dawn holds dew.
She moves with the weight of stars, unfaltering,
Each step a testament, each glance a vow unbroken.
In her embrace, I find the breath of peace,
A tender hush, a silken stillness that mends the soul.
Her words are rivers, carving deep within me,
Not to change but to soothe, steady, and stay true.
In her trust, I am a man reclaimed,
Finding courage in the faith she lends.
She is my axis, my unshaken ground,
The enduring light that neither wavers nor fades.
For she is not merely the woman I love—
She is my root, my rest, my quiet absolution.

Reverence

She has become holy, a vision of quiet
divinity,
Her essence more spirit than flesh, more light
than shadow.
To look upon her is to touch the sublime,
To stand in reverence before a beauty fierce
and pure.
Her face is carved from dreams and dusk,
Her presence, a veil of grace cloaked in
mortal form.
In her laughter, I hear the hymns of ancient
realms,
And in her silence, the stillness of forgotten
heavens.
She does not walk upon earth; she drifts,

As if her soul remembers wings, as if gravity were but a suggestion.
Her hands carry the warmth of something sacred,
And in their touch, I am both whole and undone.
I am a pilgrim to her gentle mysteries,
Kneeling in the sanctuary of her gaze.
For she is both the altar and the prayer,
And I, a devout fool, am bound to her light.
I seek nothing but the gift of her presence,
Content to dwell in the radiance she spills upon the world.
She is the essence of all things beautiful, all things quiet,
A living testament to the holy that resides within us all.
For in her, I have found the heart of worship,
And in worship, I am finally, truly free.

Fervour

She is fire incarnate, a fever in my veins,
Her memory, a relentless tide that swells and burns.
Her face haunts my waking thoughts, my dreams—
A visage I cannot touch, yet cannot release.
Her name echoes like the wail of ancient winds,
A sound that drives me to the edge of madness.
Every glance of hers, every half-smile,
Etched upon the walls of my mind, indelible.
I am ensnared by her, a captive to her shadow,
Lost within a labyrinth of desire unquenched.
Her beauty is both the balm and the wound,

Her touch, a flame that sears without mercy.
I am bound, body and soul, to this fervent ache,
This love that consumes, that will not relent.
She becomes the air I breathe, yet cannot hold,
A ghost that lingers, unbidden, unbound.
There is no world beyond her, no sky, no earth—
Only her face, her voice, her scent, her fire.
I am a man made wild, untethered,
Craving her with a desperation that knows no end.
For she is both my paradise and my ruin,
And I, in my obsession, would have it no other way.

Oblivion

And now, I dissolve, surrendered to her light,
A drop of rain returning to its boundless sea.
She is no longer just woman—she is all that
breathes,
The endless song of creation, fierce and
gentle.
Her beauty is woven through my very bones,
And in her, I am both empty and whole,
broken and healed.
I have given all, abandoned all,
And in that giving, found my truest self.
She lives within me, a pulse without
beginning or end,
Her presence as intimate as blood, as vast as
sky.
In her, I have found the essence of all things,

The quiet truth that binds us to stars and earth alike.
She is the sigh of the cosmos, the breath of all that is,
And I am but a man blessed to bear witness.
For love is no longer a feeling but a state,
A silent, enduring light that knows no bounds.
We are one, woven from the same sacred fire,
A love that stretches beyond flesh, beyond time.
And in this union, I have found eternity,
A love transcendent, undying, pure.
In her embrace, I have vanished,
Yet in vanishing, I am finally home.

Numbed

The world stopped, shuddered, unraveled,
As if all light had slipped from its seams.
I stood, hollowed and undone, a mere
fragment
Caught in the silence carved by your absence.
Nothing in the air, in the earth, made sense—
The weight of reality too much to bear,
Yet too unreal to hold.
I tried to call your name, but it drifted,
Like smoke dissolving on an indifferent
breeze,
Leaving me voiceless, abandoned in shadow.
In that brittle, breathless instant,
The world stood still and tearing apart,
Like a shattered mirror refusing to fall.
You were here—weren't you?

Or was it only a dream now undone,
Leaving me stranded in its vacant after?
I reached into the emptiness,
Finding only the hollow echo of what once was,
A ghost that lingered, silent, cold.

Mirage

This cannot be the truth—no, not this.
I weave a world spun from your memory,
A place where you still breathe, still smile,
And I hold fast to that precious illusion,
Even as time itself whispers against it.
In my mind, you still walk beside me,
Your voice a river that flows through my days,
Unfading, untouched by loss or decay.
I tell myself you are only away,
Lost in a mist that will soon clear,
And I wait, foolish yet faithful,
Clinging to the sweet lie of your return.
Reality becomes a distant stranger,
A shadow I refuse to acknowledge.
For as long as I believe, you remain,
A star hidden by cloud, yet shining,

And I will not let go, cannot let go,
Of the warmth you left in this cold world.

Inferno

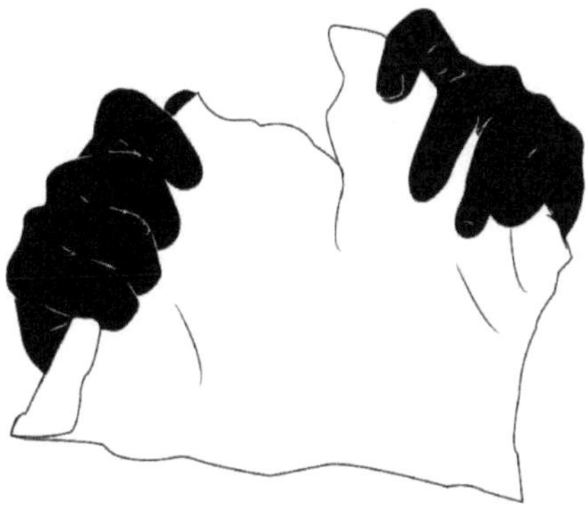

How could you leave, without a word,
Without a whisper of farewell or warning?
I rage at the sky, the earth, the stars,
At every silent thing that bore witness and did nothing.
The world mocks me with its indifferent beauty,
Its unmoved rivers, its ceaseless dawns,
And I am left, raw and raging,
A soul set ablaze in the cold of your absence.
My heart pounds with the fury of unanswered questions,
And I curse the heavens that let you slip away.
There is no justice in this, no sense, no peace,
Only the fire that burns and burns,

Scorching the space you once filled with light.
I resent the air for daring to breathe,
The stars for shining without you,
As though the universe itself betrayed us,
Left me forsaken in a world that knew no mercy.
Anger becomes my companion, fierce and unforgiving,
The only warmth I have left in this empty night.

Whisper

If only I could turn back time,
Unravel the moments that led us here,
I would hold you tighter, keep you near.
I offer silent promises to the vast, indifferent dark—
Take my days, take my years, take all of me,
If only to see you once more,
If only to bring back what has been taken.
I plead with fate, with stars, with unseen gods,
Seeking some trade, some truce,
A way to rewrite this fractured story.
Let me be the one to bear this pain,
If it means you remain untouched, unbroken.
I would trade laughter, joy, even hope itself,

For one more chance, one more moment,
To look into the eyes that gave me life.
But the silence swallows my words whole,
And I am left with empty hands and hollow prayers,
An unyielding ache that no bargain can mend.

Hollowed

Now the weight of sorrow descends, heavy as stone,
An endless dusk seeping into the marrow of my bones.
I am a husk, emptied of joy, of light, of warmth,
Wandering through the ruins of what we were.
Your absence fills the air, thick and suffocating,
And I am left adrift in a sea of shadowed thoughts,
Each one a reminder of a world you no longer breathe in.

The days blur, the nights stretch long and bleak,
I am lost in a void too vast for words,
An ocean without end, without horizon.
Nothing stirs me, nothing calls me awake—
The colors have bled from this once-vivid life,
Leaving, a soul weighed by the ashes of memory.
Your face haunts me in the quiet hours,
And I sink further into a grief so deep,
It feels as though I may never rise.
This sadness is the shadow I wear,
And I am a stranger to myself,
Broken, silent, resigned.

Resilience

When it's tumultuous outside,
The winds wrestling with the trees,
We'll sit by the window sill,
Holding a cup of coffee;
You'll draw faces on the fogged-up window
shield,
Some happy, some sad,
And laugh away looking at them.
And I, being a hopeless dreamer
Would wonder what I've done to deserve that
smile.
You'll look at me, twitching your fingers,
While I'll gaze at you, fixedly
Lost in trance of the most beautiful creation
ever.

These things make me yearn for you even more,
Like the dry winter leaves yearn for the blooming spring,
Or the scorched earth gasping for a droplet of water,
On a hot summer's day.

Words flow like water
But when you're gone,
There'll be this enormous void,
My trials of being alone.

You know, some people are irreplaceable.
And for them, we'll ignore a hundred knocks on our doors,
Of unknown faces claiming our hearts.
They'll go away,
They won't hear from me,
But this void will still be there,
A wound that can't be cured.

All I hear now is a couple of machines,
Buzzing audibly in repetitive motions.
These sounds make me uncomfortable.

Now, these thoughts will cease,
As if you never existed,
For all I've known about life,
People leave us at our worst.
Or maybe, it's the worst because they leave us.

Emergence

From the depths of loss, a seed of life emerges,
fragile yet persistent, a whisper of becoming.
There is beauty still, though faint, like dawn unfurling,
and I find, in the smallest of things, a quiet promise.
The world, though reshaped by grief, breathes anew,
its colors returning, softer, gentler, yet real.
I feel you in the laughter of strangers,
in the warmth of sunlight after rain,
and I know, somehow, you are woven through it all.
The pain does not vanish; it lives, a shadow, a truth,

but it shares its space with something bright,
a future trembling with potential.
I carry you forward, not as weight but as
wings,
for your memory now feeds this new light
within.
With each step, I find a piece of myself
restored,
not whole, yet healing, not as I was but
becoming.
And though I walk this path alone,
I am led by the gentle flame of love endured,
a hope that guides, that breathes, that lives.
In the aftermath of loss, life rises again,
and I, once shattered, rise with it,
transformed.

Embrace

The sea waves embrace a paradox of myriad proportions.
You see them far from their vicinity,
So calm, composed, prancing on the golden rays,
Or bathed in darkness under the moonless night,
The sweet sound of the waves crashing on the shore,
Tempting you to witness the happiest union you'll ever see.

When you walk along the shore,
You see the waves rushing in,
Kissing your feet gently.
She won't tell anybody

That you had walked there,
For she would wash away your footprints
And take them with her
Like they're hers.

That's where serenity marries commotion,
A seemingly tranquil wave falls for the shore,
Like two past lovers,
Detached from one another's touch,
And in an instant, dissolve into the sand,
Leaving back bubbles, swept off by the wind.

The sea is a witness to a multitude of such stories,
Stories that weave emotions
Detached from the human world,
Stories that end every moment while announcing another one,
Stories we'll never hear,
Because no one speaks of them.

Suture

Time, the slow surgeon, works without haste,
pressing its gentle fingers against tender wounds,
sewing up each tear with threads of soft memory,
turning scar into story, fracture into form.
There is an art to healing, a quiet kind of strength,
in learning to wear the scars without shame,
to let them remind me of the lessons held there,
etched deep into skin, like whispers of the past.
In the silence of solitude, I find a balm,

a stillness that cradles me as I relearn
how to hold myself, how to breathe again
without the weight of what once was.
With each day, I weave myself whole,
tending to each wounded seam with care,
until my heart, steady and scarred,
learns the quiet resilience of mending.
This heart, stitched and worn,
carries within it a strength unknown,
each healed seam a testament
to the beauty found in survival,
to the courage needed to bear
the marks of a love that once shattered,
and the grace to begin anew.

Benediction

Forgiveness, a river that flows unseen,
winds through the valleys of past pain,
softening the stones hardened by sorrow,
washing away shadows that cling to the shore.
There is no map to navigate this terrain,
no clear path to release what was,
only the gentle resolve to lay down the weight
of old grievances, of sharp-edged memories.
In this quiet benediction, I find peace—
not absolution, but acceptance of our shared
humanity.
I touch the places that hurt and offer grace,
anointing the bruised remnants of trust

with a gentleness I never knew I could
summon.
It is not an easy thing, to forgive,
to stand before the wreckage of dreams
and bless the ruins that remain.
But here, in this act of release,
I find a strange kind of freedom,
a lightness that lifts with each step forward.
The past recedes, like shadows in dawn's
wake,
and I move, unburdened and whole,
blessing the ache, the lessons, the love,
in the quiet, sacred offering of forgiveness.

Rebirth

In the warmth of a gaze that lingers just a little longer,
in the tentative reaching of two hands across distance,
trust blooms—slowly, like spring's first touch.
It is a delicate thing, fragile and new,
yet rooted deeply, nurtured by soil softened by patience.
With each step taken, cautious and sure,
the scars fade, the walls crumble,
and a tender foundation begins to form.
Trust, once shattered, now glimmers faintly,
rekindled by hands that bear the weight of hope,
by hearts willing to risk the sharp edges of vulnerability.
The soil remembers, holds every seed,

and from the ashes of yesterday's pain,
a fresh bloom rises, unfurling with quiet
grace.
I look into your eyes, finding a reflection
of all that we lost, and all that we reclaimed.
In this gentle rebirth, we find each other
anew,
not as we were, but as we are—
stronger, braver, shaped by the storms,
yet softened by the light that followed.

Convergence

We speak in silences that echo deeper
than words could ever reach, a quiet language
of souls
meeting once more across a landscape both
familiar
yet strange, raw and profound in its honesty.
Here, in the quiet between breaths, we linger,
no need for explanations, no need for
apologies.
Our past is written in the spaces we share,
each pause, each glance a testament to truths
left unspoken.
There is a closeness, an intimacy reborn,
not in grand gestures, but in the stillness,
in the way we inhabit this fragile now.

I trace the lines of your presence,
the curve of memory meeting the edge of
reality,
as though the past were a dream we both
dreamed,
and this, our reawakening.
In you, I find a mirror—
the reflection of all I am, and all I could be.

Reawakening

As we drive across the mountains,
The asphalt shimmers hot under the wheels,
Your scarf swaying to the tune of the winds
And your favorite song on the radio;

We unlock a new destination,
Where the path uncurls itself from sleep,
Slowing down at each approaching curve.

People disappear in a cloud of smoke,
Just as they always have.
This temporal world won't listen
To our cries.

They're strangled by their own thoughts—
Thoughts that bind people
In the name of freedom.
And so, they wait for eternity,
For death to come.

It's colder up here,
The breeze tussling your hair
Like a child at play;
The voices recede
And smoke bellow up
From the unknown crevices of the mountain.

So that's how things begin;
We leave our stories behind,
Safe among the woods,
Where they'll whisper to themselves,
On every dawn,
How the two of us,
Strived against the world,
And now we're free,
Not belonging to anywhere,
Yet claiming the whole world as ours.

Elysium

Here, we rest—not in flawless bliss,
but in the sanctuary of truth,
where every scar tells a story,
each silence a bond we need not name.
Our love is woven from threads of
endurance,
a tapestry stitched by hands that trembled,
yet refused to let go.

We sit in this quiet eternity, side by side,
not as we were, untested and unmarked,
but as those who have weathered storms,
borne the weight of shadows,
and still seek the light in each other's eyes.

You are no stranger, yet no longer the
same—
you are the soul that mirrors my own,
deepened by all that we have carried.

In this place of gentle knowing,
we need no grand gestures, no
proclamations,
for love is quiet here, resting in breath,
in the space where my hand finds yours
and holds it, with the strength of all we've
been.
Together, we trace the fault lines of our past,
fingers soft on old wounds,
not to mourn, but to honor,
to remember the journey that brought us
here.

Here, love is both fierce and tender,
a choice made each day, a vow unspoken.
It is the patience to weather the silence,
the courage to bare each broken part.
In the softness of your gaze, I see it—
our Elysium, not perfect, but real,

a haven shaped by hands that chose to
rebuild.

And so, we linger in this quiet forever,
not bound by what was, nor by what must
be,
but simply here, in the warmth of now,
two souls held steady by the promise of
presence,
the trust woven into each breath and glance.
In you, I find my place of rest,
not as an ending, but as a beginning,
an eternal unfolding, tender and true.

Echoes of Solitude

1. Stillness

There is a silence that stretches like an endless plain,
Vast and unmapped,
Where every step echoes back, asking questions.
I sit within it,
Not as a guest but as something older—
A fragment of the quiet itself.
The air does not move,
And yet it feels alive,
Vibrating with an energy unnamed.
The walls hum softly,
Whispering their murmurs, low and ancient.

I trace my breath,
Its rise and fall
Like a tide pulling me inward.
In this stillness,
I feel the weight of things unsaid,
The shape of thoughts too raw for words.
Time slows to a crawl,
Its hands brushing against me,
Inviting me to witness,
To exist amongst the humdrums of life,
To, for once, embrace being without purpose.
Here, the self becomes whole again—
Not by adding,
But by shedding its robes off,
Stripping of the noise,
I am nothing more than presence,
And that,
I learn,
Is everything.

2. The Empty Bench

Beneath the twisted arms of an old willow,
A bench stands alone.
The wood, weathered,
Its edges softened by the years.
It carries the weight of those who sat before
me—
Lovers whispering promises,
A mother humming to her child,
A man staring into the distance,
Waiting for something he couldn't name.
Now, it holds me,
A shadow of all its former guests.
I trace the grooves in its surface,
Each line a story it keeps
But will never tell.
The wind brushes past,

Carrying whispers from the trees,
Their leaves trembling with secrets.
I sit and wait,
Though I know not for what.
The bench offers no answers,
Only its quiet company,
Its steadfast presence.
Perhaps that is enough—
A place to pause,
To be still
In a world that rushes forward without
looking back.
And so,
I let the silence wrap itself around me,
A cocoon of calm.
The bench does not speak,
But in its silence,
I hear everything I need to.

3. Hollow Lantern

I carry a lantern,
Its glass polished to reflect the world,
But its flame long extinguished.
It swings gently at my side,
A companion to my wandering.
At night,
I lift it high,
Its hollow core catching moonlight,
Casting fractured shadows
That flicker and dance like memories.
The light is faint,
Not enough to guide,
But enough to remind me
Of what was lost.

The weight of it is strange—
Both heavy and light,
Both burden and comfort.
I wonder why I carry it,
Why I cannot let it fall.
But the answer is clear:
It is not the light I seek,
But the act of carrying,
The movement forward,
The quiet defiance of continuingEven when
the path is obscured.
The lantern will not burn again.
I know this.
And yet,
its emptiness fills me
with a strange kind of hope—
a belief that even in darkness,
there is something to hold on to.

4. Walls that Whisper

The walls around me are not empty;
they are thick with memory.
Each crack in the plaster
is a vein, pulsing with stories.
They do not confine me,
though they stand tall and unyielding.
They hold me gently,
like a parent cradling a restless child.
I press my hand to their surface,
feeling their cool solidity,
their quiet strength.
At night,
they whisper.
Not in words,
but in the faint creaks and groans
of a house settling into itself.

I imagine their voice—deep, steady, patient.
It tells me to stay,
to listen,
to let my own restlessness settle.
These walls have seen lifetimes pass.
They know the weight of silence,
the beauty of stillness.
In their quiet presence,
I feel my own edges soften.
I become not smaller,
but simpler,
my worries dissolving into the still air.
The walls whisper again,
their song soft and endless.
I listen,
and in their quiet wisdom,
I find peace.

5. The Vastness Within

Close your eyes,
and let the world unfold inward.
Beneath the surface of thought,
there is a landscape vast and untamed.
Here, mountains rise from memories,
their peaks sharp with longing.
Rivers carve through the terrain,
each curve a question unanswered.
Forests grow dense with fears,
their shadows deep and unyielding.
And yet,
beauty breathes within the chaos.
In this vastness,
I find pieces of myself
I thought I had lost.
They shine like stars scattered across a dark
sky,

small, but steady,
each one a reminder
that I am whole, even in my fragmentation.
The self is not a single thing—
it is a constellation,
a collection of moments and meanings,
woven together by time and breath.
I wander this inner world,
its vastness humbling and freeing.
Here,
I am not truly alone.
In the silence of solitude,
I hear the echoes of my own heart,
beating steady, beating strong,
a rhythm that guides me
through the endless expanse of being.

Nature's Metaphors

1. The Language of Trees

Beneath their towering canopies,
the trees whisper in a tongue
older than time itself.
Each rustling leaf
carries secrets spun by winds
that have traveled continents.
Their roots dive deep into the earth,
veins that pulse with the rhythm
of an ancient world.
I press my hand to a trunk,
its bark rough, weathered,
alive with unspoken stories.
Here lies a patience I cannot fathom—

a stillness that grows,
unhurried, undemanding.
The trees speak without sound,
their words etched in the air,
in the play of sunlight on leaves,
in the way branches sway
to the music of storms.
They are poets,
translating the language of the earth
into verses we might one day understand.
And as I stand among them,
small, transient,
I feel their gaze upon me—
gentle, knowing,
as though they have seen me before,
and will remember me again,
long after I am gone.

2. River's Tale

The river winds through the valley,
its waters silver in the morning light.
It carries the weight of time—
rain that fell centuries ago,
tears shed by those who loved and lost.
Its flow is unbroken,
a song sung in one endless breath.
I kneel at its edge,
watching its surface ripple with secrets.
It knows the contours of the land,
every rock it has polished smooth,
every grain of sand it has carried away.
The river is not just water;
it is memory,
a thread connecting the past
into the ever-shifting present.

Its voice is constant,
soft yet insistent,
reminding me that life too flows—
not in straight lines,
but in bends and turns,
shaped by its quiet resilience.
I dip my hand into its cool embrace,
and for a moment,
I am part of its story,
a fleeting current
in its endless journey.

3. Beneath the Storm

The storm arrives with a growl,
its voice rolling across the horizon.
Clouds gather like armies,
their edges dark and frayed.
The wind rises,
whipping through the trees,
pulling leaves into its wild, chaotic dance.
I stand beneath it,
unmoving, unafraid.
There is a power here—
raw, untamed,
a force that speaks of beginnings and endings.
Lightning fractures the sky,
its brilliance fleeting but unforgettable,
a reminder of how swiftly the world can
change.

The rain follows,
not as a threat,
but as a blessing.
It falls in heavy drops,
washing away the dust of days.
The earth drinks deeply,
its thirst endless,
its gratitude silent.
When the storm passes,
the air feels new,
the world brighter,
as though it has been remade.
And I, too,
feel lighter,
as though the storm has carried away
The weight of what I no longer need.

4. The Field of Seasons

The field stretches wide,
its grasses swaying in harmony with the wind.
Each season leaves its mark—
spring's gentle bloom,
summer's golden fire,
autumn's soft decay,
winter's quiet frost.
The land does not resist;
it accepts each change
with grace,
its roots drinking deeply
from the well of time.
I walk through it,
feeling the crunch of dry leaves

beneath my feet,
the whisper of seeds scattered
in the promise of another spring.
The field is not just a place—
it is a testament to resilience.
It bends but does not break,
its spirit unyielding
even in the face of winter's chill.
As I stand in its embrace,
I understand—
life, too,
is a field of seasons,
each one necessary,
each one beautiful
in its own fleeting way.

5. Mountains Know

The mountains rise in solemn majesty,
their peaks piercing the heavens.
They do not seek attention;
they simply are.
Each rock tells a story,
etched in the language of time.
The wind carves their edges,
the rain smooths their faces,
but they endure,
steadfast, eternal.
I climb their slopes,
my footsteps hesitant,
my breath shallow.
The mountain does not judge my pace,
nor care if I reach the summit.
It simply exists,
a silent witness
to the world below.

At the top,
the air is thin,
the view endless.
I see the valley stretched wide,
the rivers winding like veins.
And I realize—
the mountain is not a challenge to conquer,
but a lesson in stillness,
a reminder of the power
in simply being.

Dreamscapes

1. The Veil of Sleep

As the day's weight unravels,
I step into a realm undefined—
a threshold between the waking and the imagined.
Here, the air hums softly,
alive with whispers of forgotten places.
The veil is thin but resilient,
woven from threads of memory and longing.
It parts easily,
inviting me to wander paths unbound by time.

Mountains rise suddenly,
their peaks glowing with unearthly light,
while rivers carve silent hymns into the land.
The rules of gravity dissolve;
I float,
drawn only by the magnetism of thought.
Here, I am not a body,
but an essence,
shape-shifting as the dream wills.
Faces blur into landscapes;
words melt into color.
I reach for a tree of light,
its branches trembling under my gaze.
It bends towards me,
offering nothing but its quiet radiance.
As the veil thins at dawn's edge,
I carry fragments of this realm—
a scent, a sound,
a pulse of infinite possibility.
The dream may fade,
but its echo remains,
a soft reminder
of the worlds waiting within.

2. Labyrinth of Stars

The night sky folds inward,
its stars no longer distant points,
but a labyrinth I must traverse.
Each light calls to me,
its voice soft, melodic,
a thread woven into the vast tapestry above.
I step forward,
unsure of the ground beneath me.
The constellations rearrange themselves,
drawing maps only I can see.
They pulse with meaning,
their stories, ancient yet alive.
I follow Orion's belt,
its stars shifting as I approach.

A path opens—
a corridor of light bending endlessly.
I walk it,
not as a seeker,
but as a part of the sky itself.
My thoughts scatter,
becoming dust,
becoming stars.
At the labyrinth's heart,
there is no treasure,
only stillness,
a silence so vast it holds everything.
I close my eyes,
and the stars hum a song of return.
When I awaken,
the stars are gone,
but their song lingers,
etched into the quiet of my soul.

3. The Mirror Lake

A lake stretches before me,
its surface glass,
reflecting a sky more vivid than the real.
I kneel at its edge,
watching the reflection of myself—
a face unfamiliar yet known.
The water ripples,
breaking the illusion.
Shapes rise from its depths,
phantoms of a life forgotten.
They move with quiet grace,
whispering secrets I cannot grasp.
I dip my hand into the cool surface,
and the lake pulls me inward.
I sink,
not into darkness,

but into light, fractured and scattered.
Each shard carries a memory:
a laughter unspoken,
a touch undone,
a moment lost to time's tide.
The lake releases me,
its surface calm once more.
I rise,
my reflection clear,
yet changed.
The lake has given me no answers,
but it has shown me the depth of my own
unknowing.
The journey ends not in understanding,
but in embracing,
the beauty of questions left unanswered.

4. The Infinite Library

In a dream, I find a library—
its walls stretching beyond sight,
its shelves laden with books
bound in strange, glowing covers.
Each book hums softly,
its pages alive with words
that shift and shimmer.
I open one,
and the letters rise,
spilling into the air.
They form a river,
carrying me through memories
that are not my own.
The library is endless,
its corridors branching into infinity.
I walk through them,

guided not by direction,
but by an unseen force.
Each book I touch whispers my name,
as though it knows me better than I know
myself.
At its heart,
I find a single empty book.
Its pages are blank,
its cover warm beneath my fingers.
I lift a pen,
unsure of what to write.
The library does not demand answers;
it only offers the space to imagine.
I begin to write,
and as the ink flows,
the dream bends,
unfolding into something entirely new.

5. The Final Door

At the edge of the dream,
there is a door—
its surface smooth,
its handle cool against my palm.
It does not open easily.
I push,
and the weight of the dream resists me.
Beyond it,
there is light,
soft and golden,
flickering like a memory half-remembered.
I step through,
and the world collapses.
Colors blur,

sounds dissolve,
and I am left in a void
that is neither empty nor full.
Here, time is an echo,
a faint rhythm that pulses around me.
The door stands behind me,
closed now,
its presence a reminder of what I've left
behind.
But the void is not cold;
it cradles me gently,
its silence alive with possibility.
I am not afraid.
The door has led me here,
not as an end,
but as a beginning.
When I awaken,
the dream is gone,
but the door remains within me—
a threshold I will cross again
when the night calls me home.

Journeys Within

1. The Mapless Road

I walk a road without markers,
its surface uneven,
its edges blurred.
There are no signposts,
no paths carved by others.
Each step is an act of faith,
a conversation with the unknown.
The sky above shifts—
blue melting into gold,
then deepening into velvet dusk.
Shadows stretch and contract,

as if alive,
as if watching.
I carry nothing but questions,
their weight, both a burden and a guide.
Where does this road lead?
What waits beyond the horizon?
The road offers no answers,
only its unyielding presence.
As the journey stretches on,
I realize the road is not leading me outward,
but inward.
With each step,
a layer of doubt peels away,
revealing something raw,
something true.
The map is not drawn by others;
it unfolds with every choice I make.
And though the destination remains unseen,
the journey itself feels enough—
a testament to the courage
of moving forward
without certainty.

2. The Forgotten Room

Deep within myself,
I find a room I did not know existed.
Its walls are bare,
its corners heavy with shadows.
Dust lingers in the air,
a quiet testament
to how long it has been left unopened.
I step inside cautiously,
as though intruding upon something sacred.
The floor creaks underfoot,
each sound echoing too loud.
In the center,
a box sits,
its lid slightly ajar.

I approach it slowly,
my breath catching.
Inside,
there are fragments—
photographs faded with time,
letters penned in a hand
I no longer recognize.
These are the pieces of a self
I had left behind,
buried in the chaos of moving forward.
I hold them one by one,
letting their weight settle in my hands.
The room does not judge me;
it simply waits,
its silence a mirror to my own.
When I leave,
I carry not the fragments,
but the knowledge,
that they were always a part of me—
not lost,
just waiting to be found.

3. Voices of the Past

There is a voice that calls to me
from somewhere deep within.
It is not loud,
but it resonates,
vibrating in the hollow spaces of my being.
It speaks in a language
I thought I had forgotten—
soft syllables that carry the weight
of years lived and left behind.
The voice belongs to a self
I no longer wear,
but cannot escape.
It whispers of choices made,
paths taken and abandoned.
It does not accuse;

it simply reminds.
The past is not a shadow
that clings to my heels;
it is a foundation,
a quiet presence beneath the surface.
I sit with it,
letting its words wash over me.
There is no need to respond,
no need to push it away.
The voice fades,
leaving behind only echoes.
But in those echoes,
I hear something new—
not regret,
but understanding.
The past does not ask for forgiveness;
it only asks to be seen.

4. Through the Looking Glass

I stand before a mirror,
its surface polished and clear.
The reflection stares back—
a face I know
but do not fully recognize.
The eyes hold stories
I have yet to tell,
their depths shimmering
with questions unspoken.
I reach out,
and the glass meets me,
cool and unyielding.
For a moment,
the reflection wavers.
It becomes a kaleidoscope of selves—

child, dreamer, wanderer,
each one layered upon the other.
They merge and shift,
a dance of identity
I cannot pin down.
The mirror does not lie,
but it does not reveal the whole truth.
It shows what is,
not what will be.
And yet,
in its silent clarity,
it offers a challenge:
to look deeper,
to see beyond the surface,
but the vastness within.
When I step away,
the reflection fades,
but its gaze lingers.
I carry it with me,
a reminder that I am always more
than what I see.

5. The Hidden Garden

Within the tangle of my mind,
there is a garden
I stumble upon by accident.
Its paths are overgrown,
its flowers wild and untamed.
The air hums with life,
the scent of earth and green things
sharp and sweet.
I kneel in the soil,
my hands sinking into its cool embrace.
Here, there are no plans,
no blueprints.
The garden grows as it wills,
a testament to the chaos of creation.

In its shadows,
I find quiet.
In its bursts of color,
I see fragments of myself—
the parts that refuse to be pruned,
that thrive despite neglect.
The garden does not demand my attention,
but it welcomes it.
I stay for a while,
watching the light shift through the leaves.
When I rise,
there is dirt on my hands,
but it feels like a gift,
a mark of belonging.
The garden is not hidden;
it is simply waiting,
patient and persistent,
for me to return.

Fleeting Encounters

1. The Stranger's Smile

It happened in a moment,
a fleeting curve of the lips,
a silent acknowledgment of existence.
The stranger's smile,
so brief it felt unreal,
carried a warmth that lingered longer
than it should have.
We were passing by,
two lives intersecting
for the span of a heartbeat.
Their eyes, soft and searching,
held a quiet understanding,

as if they saw not just me,
but the weight I carried.
I wanted to ask who they were,
where they were going,
what stories their hands
would write into the world.
But the moment slipped,
the tide of time
pulling us apart.
Even now,
I think of that smile—
a flash of humanity
in an otherwise indifferent day.
It was nothing,
and it was everything.
A reminder that connection
needs no language,
only the courage to look,
to see,
to offer the smallest gift
of recognition.

2. Passing Shadows

The train station was alive with movement—
a symphony of shuffling feet,
murmured conversations,
and the occasional piercing whistle.
Among the chaos,
I noticed her—
a shadow slipping through the crowd.
She was there,
and then she wasn't,
a fleeting presence
leaving behind an ache of curiosity.
Her coat, frayed at the edges,
carried the scent of rain.
Her steps seemed purposeful,
yet lost.

I wanted to follow,
to understand who she was,
where she had been.
But she dissolved
into the sea of faces,
another ghost
in the ebb and flow of transit.
Later, I would wonder
if she thought of me too—
a stranger caught
in the periphery of her world.
But I know better.
We are all passing shadows,
colliding briefly,
then fading into the endless blur
of memory.

3. Eyes Across a Room

The room was loud—
laughter cascading like waterfalls,
voices rising and falling
in waves of conversation.
And yet,
I felt the weight of their gaze.
Across the room,
their eyes met mine—
a connection so sudden
it felt like an interruption.
It wasn't desire,
not entirely.
It was recognition,
as though we'd known each other
in another time,
another life.

I hesitated.
Would I cross the room?
Would they?
But neither of us moved.
The moment stretched thin,
fragile as spider silk,
until someone spoke to them,
pulling their attention away.
The room returned to its noise,
and I to my solitude.
But the memory of their gaze
lingers still,
a quiet haunting.
Sometimes,
a glance is all we're given—
a doorway glimpsed but never opened.

4. The Forgotten Name

We met in passing,
their name offered like a gift
I forgot to keep.
It fell from my memory
as leaves fall from trees—
quietly,
inevitably.
But their voice remains,
its timbre etched into my mind,
a faint echo
that resurfaces
when the world grows still.
I can recall the way they laughed,
how their eyes crinkled
at the corners.

I try to conjure their name,
but it slips through my grasp,
a shadow at the edge of thought.
Was it soft,
like the murmur of a stream?
Or sharp,
like the crack of frost?
The details blur,
but the feeling remains—
the warmth of their presence,
the weight of their words.
Perhaps names are unimportant,
mere symbols
for something far greater.
Still,
I wish I could call them by it,
just once,
to thank them
for the quiet beauty
of our brief encounter.

5. The Unspoken Goodbye

They didn't stay long,
but their presence
was a fire in winter—
unexpected,
comforting,
and fleeting.
We spoke in half-sentences,
our words dancing
around what we truly meant.
Their laugh—
soft, unguarded—
wrapped itself around me,

a melody I didn't know
I needed.
But the clock ticked louder
as the hours passed.
Goodbyes hovered unspoken,
their weight pressing against the air.
I wanted to ask them to stay,
to say something
that might tether them to this moment.
Instead,
we parted with smiles—
polite, distant,
already fading.
Later,
I'd replay it all—
their hand brushing against mine,
the light in their eyes,
the way they looked back
just once before disappearing
into the haze of the world.
Not all goodbyes
are meant to be spoken.
Some linger
in the spaces we leave behind,

a silence louder
than words could ever be.

Unseen Connections

1. Tides of Recognition

There are moments when I meet someone's
gaze,
and I am pulled in,
not by their features,
but by the echo of something unspoken.
Their eyes reflect a depth
that calls to something deep within me,
as though we have shared stories
without ever exchanging words.
We pass each other in the crowd,
our paths intersecting

like two rivers converging.
The current of life sweeps us along,
but there is an unspoken acknowledgment
that we are not strangers.
It is not familiarity,
not memory,
but something older—
a shared history,
written in the spaces between our breaths.
We speak in fragments,
the connection fragile but undeniable.
And though we part,
I carry with me the feeling
that we have always known each other,
that in some way,
we are bound
by an invisible thread.

2. Invisible Tapestry

There are threads that stretch between us,
woven in the unseen spaces of life.
They are not made of silk or gold,
but of moments,
of choices,
of unspoken truths that bind us in silence.
We move through the world,
touching others,
our actions rippling outward
without ever knowing the full extent
of their impact.
In the quiet,
these threads connect us,
looping and knotting
in ways we cannot fathom.
I feel the pull of it,
sometimes when I least expect it—
a word,
a gesture,
a fleeting glance
that carries the weight of something more.

We are not solitary beings,
as we often believe.
The fabric of our existence
is stitched together
by the hands of those who have come before
us,
and those who will come after.
We are threads in an eternal tapestry,
woven together by the quiet power
of unseen connection.

3. Shared Silences

There are times when words fail us,
falling away like autumn leaves,
caught by a wind we cannot control.
In those moments,
the silence between us becomes a language,
a conversation without sound,
yet deeply understood.
We do not need to speak
to understand each other.
There is a quiet language that flows
in the spaces between breaths,
in the rhythm of our shared presence.
It is not the silence of discomfort,
but one of connection.
The weight of it is not oppressive,
but light,

filling the space with something richer
than words could ever express.
In those quiet moments,
I feel the pull of something deeper—
a thread that binds us
not in words,
but in the spaces we hold for each other.
There are connections
that are never spoken,
yet always felt.

4. The Thread of Memory

Somewhere in the folds of time,
there is a moment,
a touch,
a fleeting glance,
that connects us to another.
It is not loud, or memorable,
but it stays,
woven into the fabric of who we are.
I cannot recall the exact moment
when you and I first met.
Perhaps we didn't meet at all,
but somehow,
I feel you in the air around me,

like a song I once heard
but cannot name.
Our lives have touched,
intertwined in ways we cannot see.
The memories we share,
though unseen,
breathe in the spaces between us.
Even when we are apart,
your presence lingers,
a thread pulled taut
by the weight of time.
You are not here,
but you are still with me—
woven into the tapestry
of my existence,
unseen but never forgotten.

5. The Quiet Mirror

We are mirrors,
reflecting each other in ways we cannot fully grasp.
What I see in you is not just your face,
but fragments of myself,
of what I am becoming,
of what I have left behind.
In the stillness of our exchange,
I trace the patterns,
the small pieces of me
that I have lost or hidden,
now reflected back to me through your gaze.
It is as if we are two parts of the same whole,
fragmented and searching,

trying to understand
what it means to be truly seen.
And though we may never speak of it,
the recognition is there,
a quiet understanding that transcends words.
You are both a reflection and a window,
showing me myself
and the world beyond.
In this unspoken exchange,
we find each other,
not in the clarity of our vision,
but in the tender way we reveal ourselves
through the other's gaze.

In Quiet Rebellion

1. The Unspoken No

There is power in silence,
a quiet refusal that speaks louder than words.
It is not the brash defiance
of shouting from rooftops,
but the steady strength
of standing firm
in the face of overwhelming pressure.
I have said no,
not with my voice,
but with my absence,
with my stillness,
with the way my soul
resists what does not belong.

This is not a battle fought
in daylight,
but a stirring in the deepest corners—
a rebellion against expectations,
against norms,
against everything that tries to shape me
into something I am not.
The world demands conformity,
but I stand unyielding,
in the quiet,
in the place where my truth resides.
It is a small no,
and yet it is enough.
It seeks no applause,
does not need a witness.
It simply is.
A quiet rebellion,
a small act of freedom
that defies the world's insistence
on fitting in.

2. The Quiet Fire

There is a fire within me,
though no one can see its flame.
It does not roar or crackle
or demand attention.
It is a quiet, steady burn,
a warmth that grows stronger
in the solitude of my heart.
It does not need to consume,
but to sustain.
A rebellion against the cold,
against the world that demands
I extinguish my own spark.
It is a fire of resistance,
not loud,
not forceful,

but persistent.
It keeps me going when the world tells me to stop,
when the noise outside drowns out my voice.
The quiet fire is mine,
nourished by my own choices,
my own truths.
It burns steadily in the dark,
illuminating my path,
even when no one else sees the light.
It is enough to know
that it exists,
and that it will never be extinguished.

3. The Silent Stand

I stand not in defiance,
but in stillness,
quietly holding my ground
against the rush of the world.
There is power in this silence—
a strength that does not need to be seen.
The world pushes,
presses,
demanding that I bend,
that I conform to its rhythm.
But I stand,
unmoved,
a quiet pillar in the storm.
It is not the loud resistance
that moves mountains,
but the silent resolve
that does not break.

The quiet stand is the one
that endures,
that sees the passing of time
without being swayed.
I am not visible,
not a force of loud rebellion.
I am a whisper,
a steady heartbeat
in a world that thrives on noise.
And yet,
I am enough.

4. The Hidden Voice

There is a voice inside me,
small but clear,
that rises when everything else is quiet.
It does not shout,
but speaks with a certainty
that cannot be ignored.
It is the voice of truth,
the voice of rebellion against what is
expected,
against the voices that would try to drown it
out.
It is the quiet voice that refuses to be
silenced,
that finds its way in the dark.

This voice is not loud,
it does not demand the world's attention,
but it speaks for me
when I have no words.
It speaks when I am too afraid,
too unsure,
too tired.
And when it speaks,
it is enough.
A quiet revolution in my heart,
a reminder that the truest voice
does not need to be heard
to be powerful.

5. The Quiet Departure

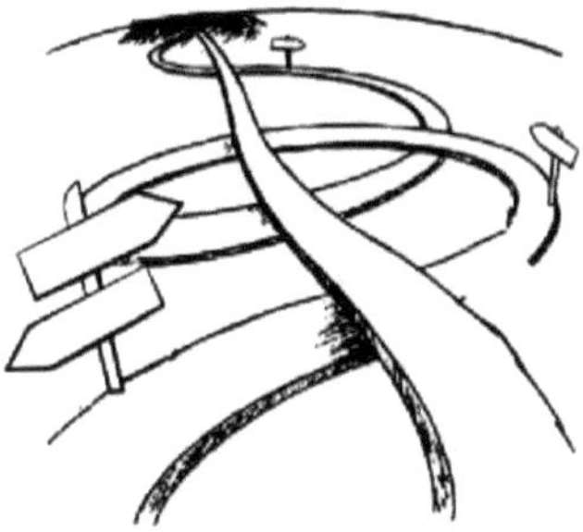

I leave not with fanfare,
but with a quiet step,
the softest of goodbyes.
There is no dramatic exit,
no doors slammed behind me.
I simply fade away,
as quietly as I entered.
The world will not notice,
at least not right away.
But I know.
I know the weight of this departure,
the courage it takes
to step away from what no longer fits.
This is not the rebellion
of a loud exit,

but the quiet one.
The one that leaves behind no traces,
no messy aftermath.
Only silence,
and the space I once occupied.
I do not need applause,
do not need recognition.
I leave because I must,
because my path leads elsewhere,
and I am no longer bound
by the ties that once held me.
A quiet departure
is its own kind of courage—
a refusal to remain
when the soul is no longer home.

The Depths of Silence

1. The Language of Silence

In the depths of silence,
there is a language we speak,
not in words,
but in gestures,
in glances,
in the spaces between breaths.
It is a language that requires no translation,
for it is felt rather than heard.
In the quiet,
we find our truest selves,

the parts of us that cannot be captured
by the limits of speech.
We communicate in the pauses,
in the way our eyes meet
without a single word.
The silence carries more than any sentence
could.
It holds the weight of unspoken
understanding,
of shared experiences
that cannot be confined to mere vocabulary.
And in this silence,
we do not need to explain.
We simply are,
and in that being,
we communicate the most.
There is power in the quiet,
in the space where words fail,
where the heart speaks
in its own untranslatable tongue.

2. The Weight of Quiet

The silence settles like a heavy blanket,
weighing down on everything,
soft but dense.
It fills the air with its presence,
not oppressive,
but undeniable.
It is not empty,
this quiet.
It carries the weight of all the things
we cannot say,
all the things that hover just beyond our
reach.
It is not an absence,
but a fullness—

a presence that takes up more space
than the loudest words ever could.
In the quiet,
we are forced to confront ourselves,
to listen to the things we ignore
when the noise drowns them out.
The silence is a mirror,
reflecting all the truths we run from,
but also offering us the chance
to face them with open eyes.
It is a silence that demands attention,
not with its loudness,
but with its weight.
And in that weight,
we find a deeper truth.

3. The Silent Depths

There are depths in silence,
hidden and unexplored,
where no words can reach.
It is a place where the mind cannot travel,
but the heart can.
In the silent depths,
we find the things that words cannot
capture—
the sorrow that lingers in the bones,
the joy that rises without sound,
the peace that settles like dew on the soul.
It is not a void,
but a space rich with meaning.
The silence holds within it
the pulse of all that has come before,
and all that will come after.
It is the place where time bends,

where memory sleeps,
and where possibility waits to be born.
In the quiet depths,
there is no need for explanation.
The silence speaks for itself,
and in its language,
we find our own truth,
our own place in the world.
It is not a silence to be feared,
but one to be embraced,
for in it,
we discover the beauty of what lies beyond words.

4. The Soundless Truth

There is a truth that is not spoken,
but simply understood.
It does not shout from the rooftops,
does not demand attention.
It is the quiet truth,
the one that settles in your chest
and remains there,
unchallenged.
It is the truth of being,
of existing without the need to explain,
of knowing that something is true
even when there are no words for it.
It is the truth that lies beneath the surface,
beneath the noise,
beneath the expectations of the world.
We try to express it,
to frame it in words,

but the silence always returns,
for no words can fully capture it.
The truth remains,
unspoken,
but always present,
like the stillness in the air before a storm,
like the calm in the heart before the world
falls away.
And in that silence,
the truth is known.
Not because we say it,
but because we feel it,
because it is.

5. The Comfort of Silence

There are moments when silence is a refuge,
a place to hide from the world
and its ceaseless demands.
In the quiet,
we find a soft embrace,
a space where we can simply exist
without needing to perform,
without needing to be anything other than
ourselves.
It is not an emptiness,
but a fullness,
a sense of being held by the stillness.
In silence, we can let go

of the burdens we carry,
the expectations that weigh us down.
There is no judgment here,
no pressure,
only the gentle presence of peace.
In the quiet,
we can breathe,
and with each breath,
we find a small piece of comfort,
a small piece of ourselves
we had forgotten.
The silence is not cold or distant,
but warm and welcoming,
a soft place to land
when the world becomes too much.
In its stillness,
we find rest,
and in that rest,
we find renewal.

The Quiet of Departure

1. The Final Goodbye

There is a silence that speaks louder than
words,
the quiet that settles in the air
before the final goodbye.
It is not the absence of sound,
but the presence of everything unsaid—
the things we leave behind
and the things we wish we had said.
In this silence,
the weight of all that has passed
hangs heavy.
The goodbye is not in the words,

but in the way we look away,
in the way we hesitate before turning the corner,
knowing that there is no turning back.
The final goodbye is a quiet one,
a moment that lasts forever
but only exists for an instant.
It is not loud,
but it is impossible to ignore.
It is the space between breaths,
the pause before the door closes,
and the heart breaks open.
And in this silence,
we understand that some departures
are not meant to be understood,
but felt,
in the quiet of the soul
that remembers long after the footsteps fade away.

2. The Weight of Leaving

Leaving is not always a choice;
sometimes it is the only way forward.
But the weight of leaving
sits heavy in the chest,
a reminder that everything we carry
has a place we must leave behind.
The world may go on,
but the pieces of us we leave behind
remain.
They settle into the spaces we vacate,
like shadows of who we were.
And with each step away,
the echoes of our past stretch out,
whispering of all we have lost.
Leaving is not an easy thing,
for it is more than a physical departure;

it is an emotional one,
a leaving of parts of ourselves
that we cannot reclaim.
But it is in this leaving
that we grow,
that we find the courage
to move forward into the unknown.
Even in the weight of leaving,
there is a lightness—
for we carry with us the lessons,
the love,
and the strength
that only departure can bring.

3. The Silent Escape

There is a quiet kind of escape,
one that is not loud or dramatic,
but soft,
like a breath that is exhaled,
then gone.
It is an escape not from a place,
but from the ties that bind us—
the expectations, the demands,
the things we have outgrown.
The silent escape is not noticed
by the world around us,
but it is felt deeply within.
It is the moment we realize
that we no longer belong,
that the place we once called home

has changed,
and so have we.
It is a departure not in the body,
but in the heart,
when we make the choice
to leave behind the things
that no longer serves us.
And in this quiet leaving,
we find freedom—
freedom to rediscover ourselves,
to find new paths
and new places to call home.

4. The Lingering Presence

Sometimes, leaving does not mean absence.
Sometimes, those who depart
linger in the quiet places,
in the spaces between moments.
They are not gone,
but remain—
in the things they left behind,
in the memories that hang in the air like a
fragrance,
in the silence that follows them.
Their presence does not shout,
but whispers,
like a shadow just beyond our reach.
We can feel them in the spaces they occupied,
in the way the world shifts when they are no

longer here.
And though they are gone from sight,
they remain in the spaces of our hearts,
where no one else can take their place.
The lingering presence is not a burden,
but a reminder—
a reminder of the love that once was,
of the paths we walked together,
of the pieces of ourselves
that they have taken with them.
And in that silence,
we find a way to carry them with us,
to hold them in the quiet
even when the world moves on.

5. The Quiet After the Storm

After the storm,
there is a silence
that stretches longer than the storm itself.
It is a silence of waiting,
of catching our breath,
of sorting through the pieces left behind.
In this quiet,
there is no rushing forward,
no pushing against what has happened.
We sit in the stillness,
feeling the weight of all that has passed.
The storm may have cleared the way,

but the quiet that follows is where we heal,
where we come to terms with the destruction,
the loss,
and the change.
The quiet after the storm is not an absence,
but a space for reflection.
It is the calm that comes
when we are no longer fighting,
when we have no choice but to listen
to the echoes of what remains.
In this silence,
we find clarity,
we find strength,
and we find the courage
to step forward again,
knowing that the storm is over,
but the quiet will stay with us forever.

The Awakening of Dreams

1. The First Glimmer

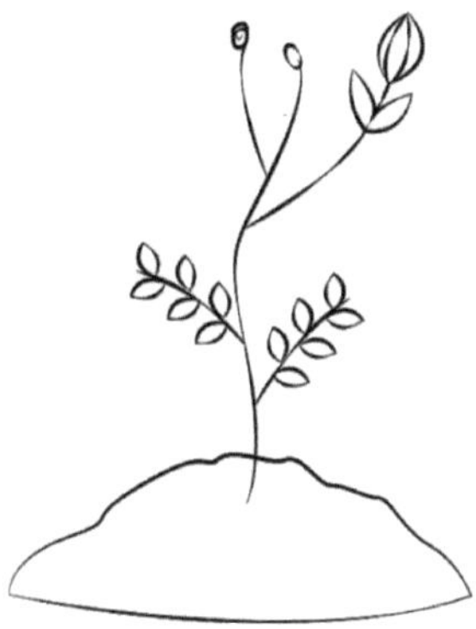

Dreams begin not as vast plans,
but as faint whispers—
a soft glimmer on the edge of our awareness.
They are the quiet hopes
that stir when we are still,
when the world fades away and we are alone
with ourselves.
It is in these moments that the seeds are
planted,
not with grand intentions,

but with the simple desire to see something
more.
The first glimmer is fragile,
easily dismissed by the noise of life.
But it is always there,
a tiny flame that waits to grow.
It does not demand attention,
but it calls to us,
urging us to listen,
to believe that there is more than what we
see.
In the quiet of that first moment,
we realize that dreams are not born from the
world outside,
but from the depths within.
They arise from the very core of our being,
carrying with them the promise of something
greater—
if we dare to follow them.

2. The Path of Courage

Dreams are not fulfilled in comfort,
but in the moments when we step into the unknown,
when we face what we fear most
and choose to keep moving forward.
The path of courage is not a straight line,
but a winding road full of uncertainty and doubt.
It is a path that demands more than we think we can give,
but rewards us with the strength to continue.
Each step on this path is a victory,
each choice to keep going a testament to our belief
in something greater than what we know.

Courage is not the absence of fear,
but the willingness to walk through it.
It is the spark that keeps the dream alive,
even when the way forward is unclear.
Without courage, dreams remain fragile,
but with it, they become unbreakable.

3. The Unseen Forces

There are forces in the world that we cannot see,
but that shape the course of our dreams.
They are not tangible,
but their presence is felt in the quiet moments of doubt,
when we wonder if we are on the right path.
These forces are the unseen hands
that push us forward when we falter,
the whispers that guide us when we lose our way.
They are not always easy to recognize,
but they are always there,
pushing us to believe in something bigger than ourselves,
something we cannot yet touch,
but that calls us to keep going.

These unseen forces are not accidents;
they are part of the dream itself,
the currents beneath the surface
that carry us when we are too tired to swim.
It is these forces that remind us
that we are not alone in our pursuit,
but that the universe conspires with us
to bring our dreams to life.

4. The Shift of Perspective

Dreams are not always what we expect them to be.
They do not always unfold in the way we imagine,
but in the way we need.
It is in the shift of perspective
that we come to understand them fully.
What seemed like an obstacle at first
becomes a stepping stone.
What once appeared as a detour
becomes the main road.
The shift in perspective is subtle,
but it changes everything.

In the midst of pursuit,
we are often so focused on the end goal
that we miss the beauty of the journey.
But when we allow ourselves to see
differently,
the dream no longer feels distant;
it becomes a part of who we are.
In that shift,
we realize that the dream was never just
about the destination,
but about the person we became
along the way.

5. The Awakening Soul

There comes a moment in every dreamer's life
when the soul awakens to its true calling,
when all that has been longed for,
all that has been hoped for,
is suddenly clear.
It is not a sudden revelation,
but a quiet knowing that rises from deep
within,
a recognition that this is the path we were
meant to walk,
the journey we were destined to take.
In that moment,
everything falls into place.
The pieces we have spent so long searching for
are suddenly here,
and we understand that all our struggles,

all our uncertainties,
were simply the preparation
for this awakening.
The awakening soul does not look to the
world for validation;
it looks within,
knowing that the only approval needed
is its own.
And in that knowing,
we finally begin to live the dream
we have carried all our lives.

Printed by Libri Plureos GmbH in Hamburg,
Germany

9 789369 545131